URBAN STRUCTURING

STUDIES OF ALISON & PETER SMITHSON

Studio Vista: London
Reinhold Publishing Corporation: New York

ACKNOWLEDGEMENTS

Most of the photographs in this book are by Nigel Henderson, others are tear sheet from magazines and the owners of the copyright are unknown. Should any copyright have been infringed, the owners are asked to write to the Publishers who will gladl reimburse them.

A large part of this book was previously published under the title of UPPERCASE 3 by Whitefriar Press as a limited edition in 1960, designed and edited by Theo Crosby

Certain illustrative material in this publication first appeared in essays published *Architectural Design.*

Berlin competition plan and Scharoon's axonometric drawing are copied from the official document of the competition: Hauptstadt Berlin Ergebnis des Inter nationalen Städtebaulichen Ideenwettbewerbs.

oele in 76556
10-1-79 BCP

A Studio Vista/Reinhold Art Paperback
Edited by John Lewis
© Alison and Peter Smithson 1967
Published in London by Studio Vista Ltd
Blue Star House, Highgate Hill, N 19
and in New York by Reinhold Publishing Corporation
a subsidiary of Chapman-Reinhold, Inc.
430 Park Avenue, New York
Library of Congress Catalog Card Number 67-27747
Set in 9/10 Univers Medium (Monotype Series 689)
Printed in the Netherlands
by N.V. Drukkerij Koch & Knuttel, Gouda
289.27861.9 Paper edition
289.27764.7 Hardcover edition

4

CONTENTS

INTRODUCTION

This is not a mere catalogue of the works of two brilliant young architects, but the presentation of a set of ideas about architecture and town planning.

These ideas have developed out of the general theory of modern architecture, modified to accomodate an entirely new economic and social situation.

Briefly, the modern movement was the product of nineteenth century rationalism and the urge for social improvement. It was essentially a move towards integration: to use the forces of society, industry and the arts in a coherent and harmonious way. Thus the nineteenth century preoccupation with style was ignored and architects became interested in method, organization and technology. In the twenties this urge found expression in the work of Walter Gropius (in the Bauhaus and later in his famous housing schemes), in J. J. P. Oud in Holland, and particularly in the polemical writing and buildings of Le Corbusier in Paris. Gropius spoke of teamwork (as opposed to the 'star' architect), Oud of standardization, Le Corbusier of technology and many other things. This was an heroic period, of many individual efforts in many countries, yet the buildings looked very similar. It was the beginning of a new architectural language.

In 1929 these few individuals founded the Congres' Internationaux d'Architecture Moderne (CIAM). The crystallization of theory into doctrine was under way. In 1933, at the CIAM congress at Athens the Athens Charter was formulated. It was a classic document. It influence was to spread all over the world. At the time the major problem facing planners was poverty and slum clearance (remember those dark documentaries full of poetry and coal miners), and the clean rationalism of minimum housing, efficient mass transport segregation of industry and creation of wide park areas which the charter implied, was a good sharp tool. In fact here was a vision of new city, of which we have built segments all over the world for the last twenty years.

The war did not destroy *this* city; that was left for the peace. Reconstruction brought problems the planner found himself without the theoretical equipment to solve, and subsequent prosperity has him on the hop. He applied the Athens Charter formula where he could we can now assess the results—in the New Towns, the City of London, and in vast areas of the Continent. By 1951 it had already become clear that the really important thing had slipped away. We were rehousing people, but the life they were expected to live was not only dreary but already socially obsolete. Condemning the New Towns became a popular sport, but as they were an economic success nothing could (or can today for that matter) move the authorities into investigating alternative housing methods.

Alison and Peter Smithson won a competition in 1951 (for a secondary school at Hunstanton) and earned a little time to think about the problem. They made friends with Eduardo Paolozzi (sculptor) and Nigel Henderson (photographer) whose wife Judith was a sociologist in Bethnal Green. Henderson was fascinated by the rich community life of his neighbours. Here was the element missing in the new towns—the close relationships of people to each other and to their environment.

The CIAM congress at Aix-en-Provence in 1953 saw the first crack in the theoretical solidity of the modern movement. The Smithsons showed Henderson's pictures, met Candilis (who had produced some remarkable Moroccan housing), J. B. Bakema of Holland and several young men who also found the Athens Charter obsolete. They formed a group to exchange information. This group, Team 10, was entrusted by CIAM to prepare the programme for the 10th CIAM congress at Dubrovnik in 1956 (apparently on the principle: if you can't beat them, join them). The method of analysis for the projects submitted was, roughly, in terms of human association rather than functional organization, thus marking a radical break in architectural thinking.

At Dubrovnik it became evident that CIAM, with over 3,000 members, had become too diffuse to cover any subject other than by the merest generalization. There was also a cleavage between the founders, old, famous and very busy, and the followers, young, underworked and ravenous for power. The congress broke up leaving Team 10 in possession of the field. Most national groups dissolved themselves. Team 10 continued to meet, at Doorn (1954) and Otterloo (1959), but they met as individuals.

Thus at the beginning of the sixties we are at the end of a movement and the beginning of its successor. Today almost every student is trained 'in the modern movement', the institutes are presided over by 'modern' architects. But we are far from a modern architecture. Most contemporary building is banal, because after watering down the formal content for twenty years little is left. Yet the modern movement also carries the seeds of its resurgence, in its insistence that the solution to any problem is to be found within the terms of the problem itself. It is here that the Smithsons' contribution has become important. They have worked steadily to extend their grip on the problem of environment. Architectural and planning competitions have provided an opportunity to work in many scales— from the house to the metropolis. On the following pages the process of their development has been compressed and, I hope, made comprehensible.

Theo Crosby, 1960 and 1967

This is a record of a search.

No attempt has been made to eliminate from the studies documented here conclusions and opinions which we do not now regard as completely valid. It is felt to be more important to leave in apparent contradictions than to eliminate steps which are necessary to an understanding of the processes and intentions of the whole.

The studies fall naturally into five groups:

ASSOCIATION   IDENTITY   PATTERNS OF GROWTH

CLUSTER   MOBILITY

These headings not only represent the content of the studies, but their order is that of the natural chronology of the idea. They are also the key-words of the new concept.

The 'life-of-the-streets' in these pictures is a survival from an earlier culture—and a subsistence culture at that. But we have not yet discovered an equivalent to the street form for the present day. All we know is that the street has been invalidated by the motor car, rising standards of living and changing values. Any revival is historicism. In the uninhibited organization of the children's games we are seeing a valid pattern, and in this is an indication of a freer sort of organization. Photographs by Nigel Henderson.

PATTERNS OF
ASSOCIATION

The main work on which the first two sections are based is the Golden Lane project (a competition for high density housing in the City of London) which was made in 1952. This scheme was elaborated into a general theory and presented to CIAM 9 at Aix-en-Provence in 1953 at which the words ASSOCIATION and IDENTITY were introduced into architectural thinking.

Some understanding of the problems of human associations which were necessary for this study was gained during visits to the house of Judith and Nigel Henderson in Bethnal Green from 1950 onwards. The Doorn Manifesto was written in 1954. It was, as it were, a declaration of war on the established methods of thinking on housing and town planning.

In a tight knit society inhabiting a tight knit development such as the Byelaw Streets there is an inherent feeling of safety and social bond which has much to do with the obviousness and simple order of the form of the street: about 40 houses facing a common open space. The street is not only a means of access but also an arena for social expression. In these 'slum' streets is found a simple relationship between house and street.

How would people use 'good' environment? How many of the traditional acts of expression (of joy, time passing, faith, play-teaching) are likely to continue to want to find expression?

Hearth and doorstep are symbols which used together present to most men's minds the image of house.

40 or 50 houses make a good street.

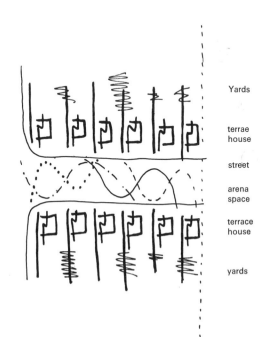

Yards

terrae
house

street

arena
space

terrace
house

yards

Streets, with many small local and some larger facilities in the interstices and round about make up a fairly recognisable district. Districts, interpersed with many more complex facilities than they would individually support, make up a city.

House, Street, District are 'elements of city'.

Housing groups being built when this breakdown of Elements of City was first proposed (in 1952), were to high standards of construction and met the needs of society as outlined by official sociologists but they lacked some very vital quality; a quality which was undoubtedly necessary in order to achieve *active* and *creative* grouping of houses. This missing quality—essential to mans' sense of wellbeing—was IDENTITY.

It was possible to recognise *identity* in parts of old housing groups. (But it was also recognised that to many, the suburban semi-detached house represents the highest attainable degree of identity.)

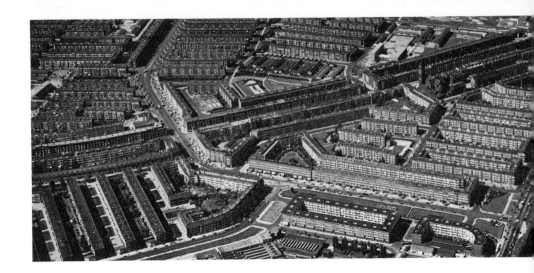

It seemed that through the very success of CIAM's* campaignir
we were now faced with inhuman conditions of a more subtle ord
than the slums.
The planning technique of the Charte d'Athene was analysis
functions. Although this made it possible to think clearly about tt
mechanical disorders of towns it proved inadequate in practi
because it was too diagrammatic a concept. Urbanism considere
in terms of the Charte d'Athene tends to produce communities
which the vital human associations are inadequately expressed.

It became obvious that town building was beyond the scope
purely analytical thinking—the problem of human relations fi
through the net of the 'four functions'. In an attempt to correct th
the Doorn Manifesto proposed: 'to comprehend the pattern
human associations we must consider every community in
particular environment.'

* 'Can Our Cities Survive?'

1 It is useless to consider the house except as a part of a community owing to the inter-action of these on each other.

2 We should not waste our time codifying the elements of the house until the other relationship has been crystalised.

3 'Habitat' is concerned with the particular house in the particular type of community.

4 Communities are the same everywhere.
   (1) detached house—farm.
   (2) Village.
   (3) Towns of various sorts (Industrial. Admin. Special).
   (4) Cities (multi functional).

5 They can be shown in relationship to their environment (Habitat) in the Geddes valley section.

6 Any community must be internally convenient—have ease of circulation, in consequence whatever types of transport are available, density must increase as population increases, i.e. (1) is least dense (4) is most dense.

7 We must therefore study the dwelling and the groupings that are necessary to produce convenient communities at various points on the valley section.

| 1 | 2 | 3 (a) | 4 | 3 or (b) (c) | 2 | 1 |

8 The appropriateness of any solution may lie in the field of architectural invention rather than social anthropology.

Much of the social pattern as observed by the sociologist in the Bye law Street is a survival—modified by the particular built environment —of even earlier patterns. There is no point in perpetuating this way of life, but it might be worth looking further back to its roots, to gain a picture of the development of a particular society.*

The aim of urbanism is comprehensibility. That is, clarity of organiza tion. The community is by definition a comprehensible thing, and comprehensibility should therefore be a characteristic of the parts The community sub-divisions might be thought of as 'appreciated units'. An appreciated unit is not a 'visual group' or a 'neighbour hood', but a part of a human agglomeration which can be 'felt The appreciated units must be different for each type of community Its scale must increase with the scale of the community. A large community cannot be built up from appreciated units evolved for small community under different conditions (e.g. houses round square). For each particular community one must invent the structur of its sub-division.

The architect-urbanist should not be blind to the fact that the patter of human associations may in certain countries turn out to be pattern of dis-association. Association does not necessarily mea contact.

Association is present even in a lighthouse through the basi means of communication: wireless, mail, the Press, the gramo phone, TV. At the hamlet and village start the second line of com munication, of impersonal association—the cinema. Through thes channels the forces of the outside world reach everybody.

Such a hierarchy of association can be expressed in a diagram.

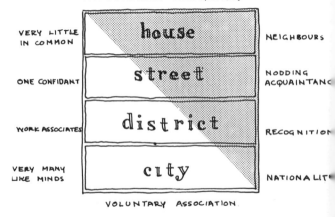

We accept as basic the individual urge to identify himself with his surroundings—with familiar objects and familiar symbols.

This study is concerned with the problem of identity in a mobile society. It proposes that a community should be built up from a hierarchy of associational elements and tries to express the various levels of association—the house, the street, the district, the city. It is important to realize that the terms used, street, district, etc., are not to be taken as the reality but as the idea, and that it is our task to find new equivalents for these forms of association for our non-demonstrative society.

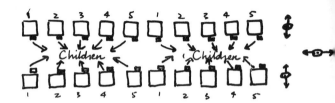

'Cars, telephones,—represent not so much a newer and higher standard of life as a means of clinging to something of the old. Where you could walk to your enjoyment you did not need a car.' Family and Kinship in East London, Young and Wilmot.

There should be a basic programme for the dwelling in terms of the activities of the family, considering them individually and in association with each other. (THE HOUSE)

The dwelling thought of in terms of human association should take account not only of the family but also those additional responsibilities which vary in all countries and with all families—this additional activity gives identity to the dwelling and its inhabitants.

Traditional Street considered as active environment is now being changed by increased mobility.

Re-identifying man with his environment cannot be achieved by using historical forms of house-groupings: streets, squares, greens etc., as the social reality they represent no longer exists.

The principle of identity we propose is the basis of the Golden Lane Project—a multi-level city with residential streets-in-the-air.

Outside the house is the first point of contact where children learn for the first time of the world outside. Here are carried on those adult activities which are essential to everyday life—shopping, car cleaning, scooter repairs, letter posting. (THE STREET)

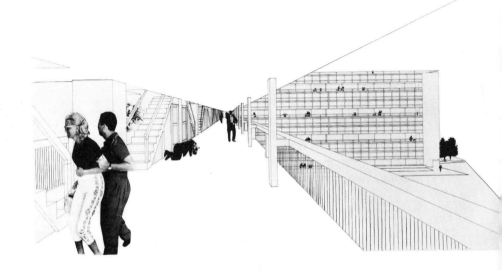

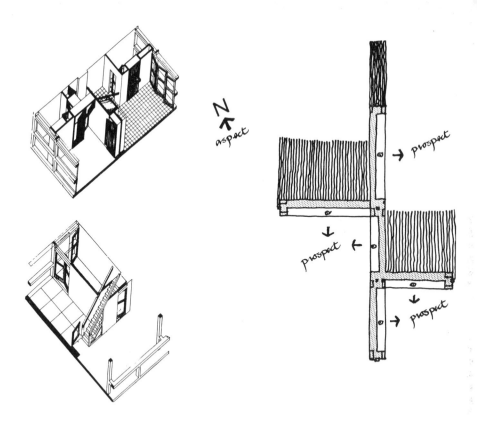

N
aspect

prospect

prospect

prospect

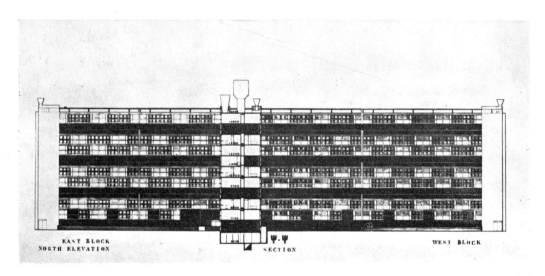

EAST BLOCK
NORTH ELEVATION

Ψ-Ψ
SECTION

WEST BLOCK

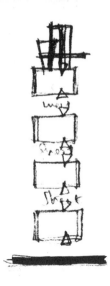

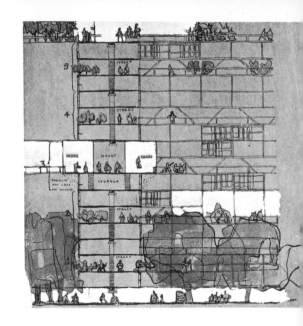

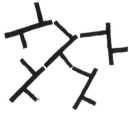

Off the street 'deck', accessed from it and the house, is the extension to the dwelling—the 'yard-garden'. The ever changing vignette patterns of sky and city seen through the yard-gardens from the ground and from the street deck itself enhance the passing stranger's view.

The street decks are intended as ample spaces, wide enough for two mothers with prams to stop to talk and still to leave room to pass. A more complex geometry than 'rational lot division' answers to the need for an environment active and creative socially. Outside the street people are in direct contact with the larger range of activities which give identity to the community. (THE DISTRICT)

Even in a small town compactness is essential. With loosely organized quarters, each associated with a certain sort of work— banking, docks, shipping concerns, furs—and varying in height and density to suit their needs, the complex would rise finite in the fields, with the uneven skyline and defined boundaries of an Italian or Greek hill town.

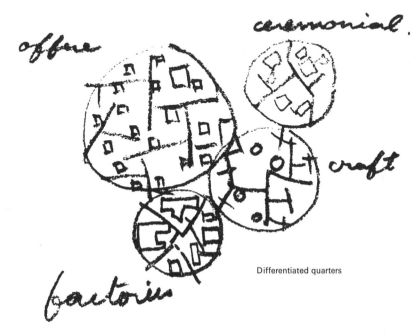

Differentiated quarters

25

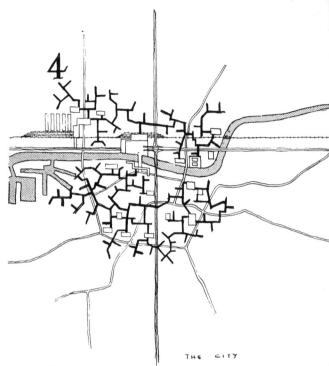

THE CITY

In order to keep ease of movement, we propose a multi-level city with residential streets-in-the-air. These are linked together in a multi-level continuous complex connected where necessary to work and to those ground elements that are necessary at each level of association. Our hierarchy of association is woven into a modulated continuum representing the true complexity of human associations.

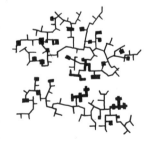

Streets-in-the-air are linked together in a multi-level continuous complex, connected where necessary to work and to those ground elements that are necessary at each level of association. Our 'hierarchy of association' is woven into a modulated continuum representing the true complexity of human associations.

Districts in association generate the need for a richer scale of activities which in their turn give identity to the ultimate community (THE CITY)

Any new combinations of dwellings with their immediate access that would make for a new way of living in the city must nearly always expect to have to lace-in between existing buildings and mesh over existing road and service networks. Their function is renewal; of the dying centres and derelict areas among railway

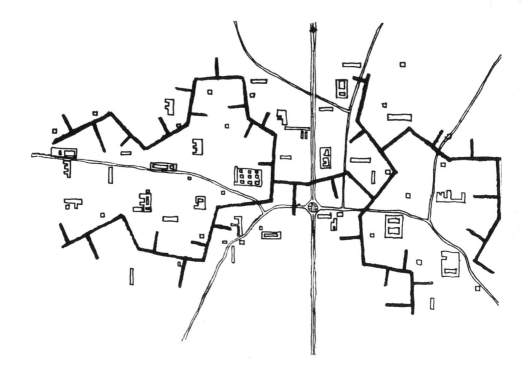

viaducts and old industrial sites. The 'elements' can expect little help from their surroundings in terms of environment but must by their unblemishable newness carry the whole load of responsibility for renewal in themselves.

The horizontal street mesh would slot into the vertical circulation of other buildings in an attempt to fuse many different kinds of multi-level buildings already in existence (offices, department stores,

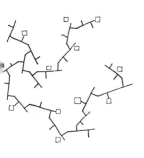

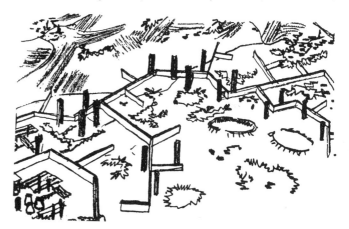

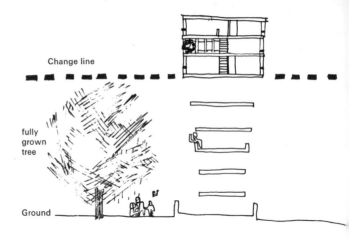

Change line

fully
grown
tree

Ground

parking garages) ; to make a city conceived as a cluster of population
pressure points, not an abstract pyramid of density figures. Such
an idea offers, 'a germ of a city convincingly urban, many valued,
growing—not one valued, fixed, and closed in a single hierarchy of
forms'.

ECOLOGICAL TABLE

GROUND		SPACE	
Parks, greens, and market gardens		Those things that are necessary to the life of the street :—	
		Workshops	
Horizontal industry		Offices	
		Hotels	
Places of assembly and ceremonial		Public terraces	
Shopping			
Road	interchanges service stations transit storage stations	Street	parking all pedestrians hand vehicles
Rail	sidings goods yards	Space	new lifts
Air	major airfields	Air	helicopters hoppycopters
Water	rivers canals estuaries, docks		

The studies of Association and Identity led to the development of systems of linked building complexes which were intended to correspond more closely to the network of social relationships, as they now exist, than the existing closed patterns of finite spaces and self-contained buildings. These freer systems are more capable of change and, particularly in new communities, of mutating in scale and intention as they go along.

It was realized that the essential error of the English New Towns was that they were too rigidly conceived, and in 1956 we put forward an alternative system in which the 'infra-structure' (roads and services) was the only fixed thing. The road system was devised to be as simple as possible and to give equal ease of access to all parts. This theme of the road system as the basis of the community structure was further explored in the Cluster City idea between 1957 and 1959, in the Hauptstadt Berlin Plan 1958, and in the London Roads Study 1959.

Principles of Town Development

A town is by definition a specific pattern of association, a pattern unique for each people, in each location, at each time. To achieve this specific pattern it must develop from principles which give the evolving organism consistency and unity.

A *town-plan* can be defined as the method of applying those principles.

The realization of the *actual* town should be in the hands of the builders of the parts, who, understanding the general intention, must at every stage assess what has gone before and by their activities mutate (if necessary re-direct) the whole.

In building a new town the nature of the first area built will be quite different to subsequent areas. Any all-over plan must have the necessity for change built in to its processes. The existing sort of Municipal Planning tries to create a pattern in advance of circumstances—it lays out the form of the new community as a finished object. This, of course, is impossible, for form is generated in part by response to existing form, and in part in response to the Zeitgeist of the period—which cannot be preplanned. Every addition to a community, every change of circumstance, will generate a new response. An aspect of this response is *scale*—the way in which the new part is organized plastically to give it meaning within the whole complex. As the complex changes with the addition of new parts, so the scale of the parts must change so that they and the whole remain a dynamic response to each other. Scale has something to do with size, but more to do with the effect of size.

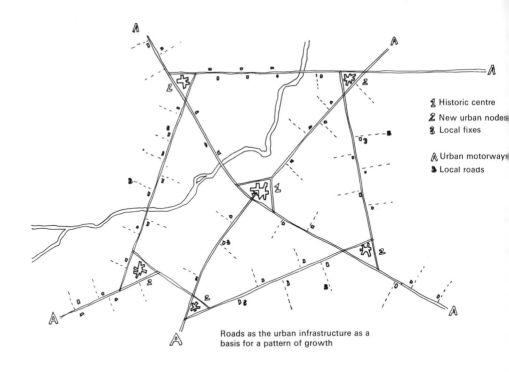

1 Historic centre
2 New urban nodes
3 Local fixes

A Urban motorways
b Local roads

Roads as the urban infrastructure as a basis for a pattern of growth

A system of urban motorways.

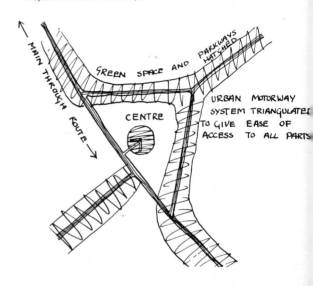

A system of road/green space.

30

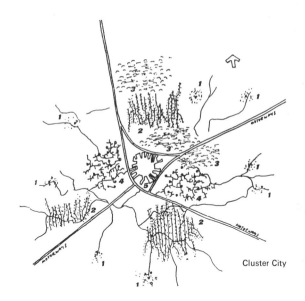

Cluster City

A city of population clusters, each working or living in types of buildings that have their own appropriate relation to motor traffic.

A system of service and communications to allow for a maximum freedom for growth and change around a clear and *indestructible* basic structure.

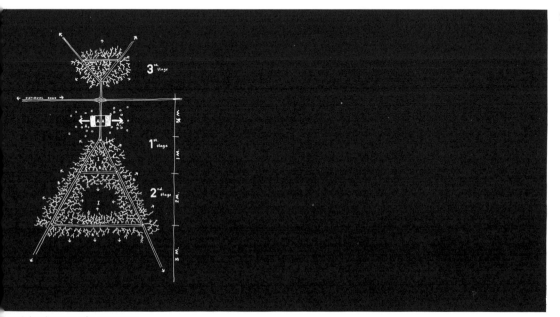

…ased development of a new town

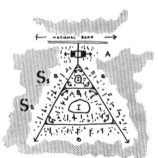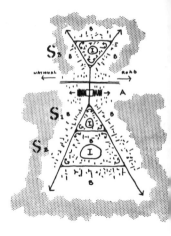

Developing town, each phase of which has an identity
Direct access to heart of city from national route. Internal road system of equilater
triangular pattern gives equal ease of access to all parts yet it is clearly orientate
Twin arteries focus on centre and pick up existing cross country roads and dire
them into town.

Similar phase development
in a building

In the complex of associations which is a community, social cc
hesion can only be achieved if ease of movement is possible. Th
assumption that a community can be created by geographic isolatio
is invalid. Real social groups cut across geographical barriers, an
the principal aid to social cohesion is looseness of groupings an
ease of communications rather than the rigid isolation of arbitra
sections of the total community with impossibly difficult commun
cations.

The concept 'patterns of growth' was applied to an actual projec
'Hauptstadt Berlin'; the idea is found in a simple form in the variou
buildings to house the Ministries. These buildings grow from th
two-storey 'Ministers' Houses'. As their attendant departments g
bigger and more anonymous so does the building that contair
them. They rise finally to high buildings (maximum 45 meters) whic
back on to an east-west road from which all office workers' cars ar
service vehicles have ingress. The Ministers and high officials con
and go by formal entries and parking spaces off a continuous 'Qua
which runs along the north bank of the Spree from Bellvue Schlo
to opposite the Dom.

The word 'cluster' was first introduced at CIAM X at Dubrovnik in 1956. The aim of Team X who organized the work for the Congress, on the lines of the Doorn Manifesto, was to demonstrate that a specific form of 'Habitat' must be evolved for each particular situation.

To make this point clear we prepared for the Congress 5 projects for particular situations. In each the pattern of development was at the same time 'free' and yet systematized. This form of organization we called the Cluster.

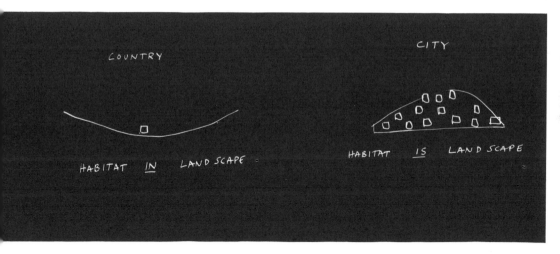

The word 'cluster', meaning a specific pattern of association, has been introduced to replace such group concepts as 'house, street, district, city' (community sub-divisions), or 'isolate, village, town, city' (group entities), which are too loaded with historical overtones. Any coming together is 'cluster': *cluster is a sort of clearing-house term during the period of creation of new types.*

Certain studies have been undertaken as to the nature of 'cluster'. The intention of these studies, in which the 'conditions' were largely made-up and not 'real', was to show in terms of actual built forms that a new approach to urbanism was possible. In other words it was to present 'an Image'. A new æsthetic is postulated as well as a new way of life.

It was necessary in the early '50's to look to the works of painter Pollock and sculptor Paolozzi for a complete image system, for an order with a structure and a certain tension, where every piece was correspondingly new in a new system of relationship.

It is our thesis that for every form of association there is an inherent pattern of building.

The first study was at the relatively simple level of association—the village. It concerned itself with 'infill'—the placing of new dwellings in and around the old village in such a way as to revalidate the existing pattern.

Typical addition to a village irrespective of location

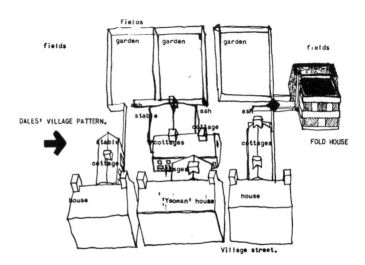

DALES' VILLAGE PATTERN.

Above : West Burton, Yorkshire
Below : village infilling all round the fringe, at the ends of the secondary access system. The new is placed over the old like a new plant growing through old branches—or new fruit on old twigs. The fold is a wind break. Each house has its back thus to the prevailing wind. This instead of the 'housing Manual' type house, sent down from the suburbs—a barrow boy on the fells.

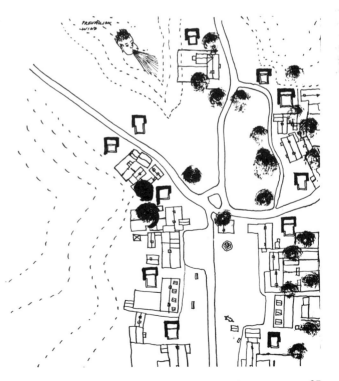

Photographed by P. H. Davis

The second study is for a new form of housing in a similar situatic
to the English New Town or a Swedish satellite neighbourhood.
Town pattern of close houses on an undulating ground retain tI
real advantages of a fresh site in the country.

The 'close' is based on an internal pedestrian way, with houses
various frontages spanning over it. A constant pitch, split to gi
top light, varies the heights with the frontages.

It is *not* a self-contained community—but relies on mobility.

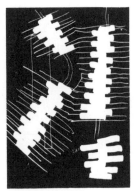

Diagram of cluster for a new
town

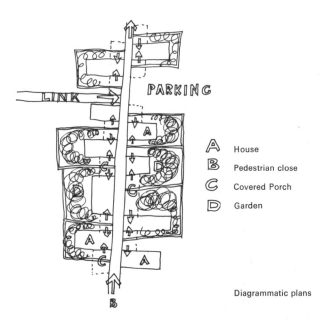

A — House
B — Pedestrian close
C — Covered Porch
D — Garden

Diagrammatic plans

Houses riding the landscape

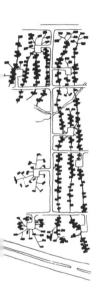

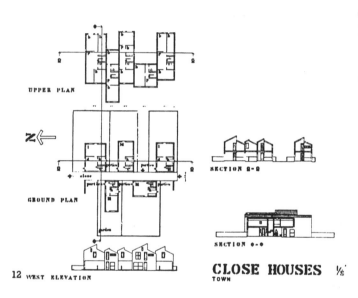

UPPER PLAN

N←

GROUND PLAN

SECTION Q-Q

SECTION O-O

12 WEST ELEVATION

CLOSE HOUSES ⅛'
TOWN

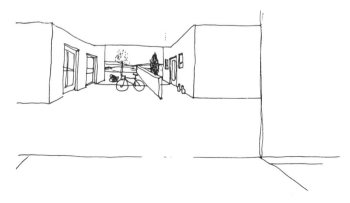

This last study, at the most complex level of association, is of infill development in an industrial quarter of a Metropolis.

The building form has sufficiently strong characteristics to make its own visual renewal order even when distributed among industrial developments at widely scattered points.

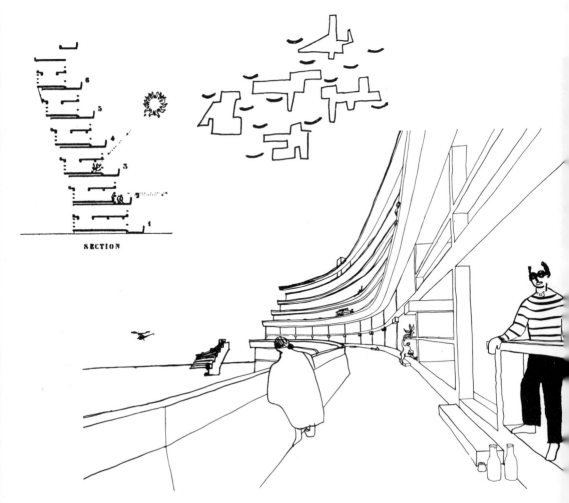

SECTION

From our first interest in the life-of-the-street we have been obsessed with the concept of 'mobility' in all its meanings, and particularly with the implications of the motor car. For the architect this is not only a matter of traffic systems for he is concerned with the invention of building types appropriate to the new urban pattern that motorization demands.

The studies in this 'record of search' concerned with building types and urban pattern in cities whose major structure is a comprehensive system of urban motorways are Hauptstadt Berlin 1958, and the London Roads Study 1959.

People and objects in motion and change are both the stuff and the decoration of the urban scene
Historical forms giving expression to different kinds of movement.

Recent images:

City of Tomorrow by Le Corbusier:

'Here we have a promenade for pedestrians rising on a gentle ramp to first floor level which stretches before us as a kilometre flight of terrace. It is flanked by cafés embowered in tree tops that overlook the ground beneath. Those hanging gardens of Semirramis, their triple tiers of terraces, are 'streets of quietude'. Their delicate horizontal lines span the intervals between the huge vertical towers of glass, binding them together with an attenuated web . . . That stupendous colonnade which disappears into the horizon as a vanishing thread is an elevated one-way autostrada on which cars cross Paris at lightning speed . . . When night intervenes the passage of cars along the autostrada traces luminous tracks that are like the trails of meteors flashing across summer heavens.'

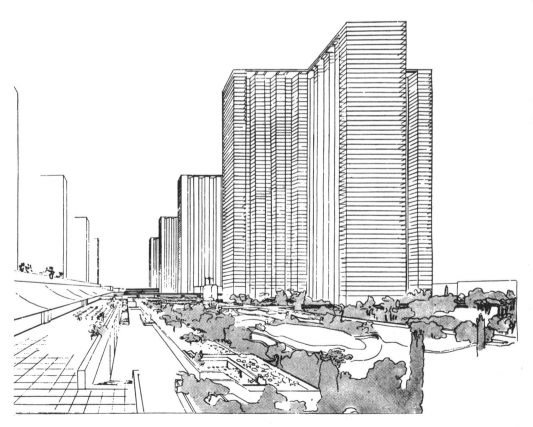

Mobility pattern built into the city form by Le Corbusier (Algiers), developed before the needs of modern transportation were understood and therefore not valid in 1960. Transportation in cities requires a network of equal value roads, not a few points to point highways, in order to equalize loadings and get maximum use of road space; also, as can be seen in the top picture opposite, the space requirements of effective interchanges are enormous. Furthermore, they need to be able to change. This is impossible if roads and interchanges are locked up with building complexes

A striking image. A dream of random ordering, but lifted from this context to that of the city a nightmare of noise and a spray of destructive energy

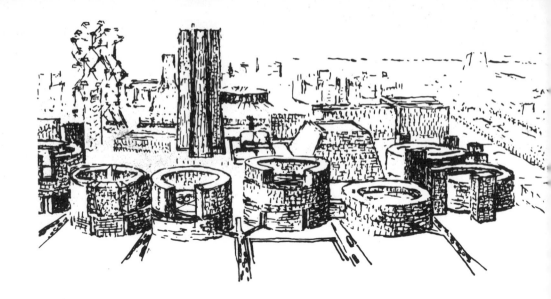

Louis Kahn owes his unique position and strength to the fact that he is the only American architect who is consciously trying to make through architecture, a re-organized and re-validated city—without any 'old hat' notions of radically changing people's way of life (or the pattern of production).

The fact that his town-planning proposals are elegant and genuinely poetic (a great rarity in planning projects for existing communities) is proof both of his tenacity, and of the basic correctness of his theories.

Meaningful order of spaces
Meaningful order of structure

Kahn's theoretical position on cities is a product of his historical insight into the fact that the qualities we admire in old cities are the product of the way that was found of giving form to the order of movement, the order of spaces for given functions and the ordering fo the structural means available so that a unique organism was created.

And his importance is not that he has said this, but that he has developed specific town-organizing techniques and architectural forms : the concept of Go Streets and Stop Streets of the Philadelphia plan, and the Town Hall Plaza of the City Center Study.

Louis Kahn on his project for Philadelphia :
'The tower entrances and interchanges, wound-up parking terminals, suggest a new stimulus to unity in urban architecture, one which would find expression from the order of movement. The location and design of these entrances are an integral part of the design of the express-way. At night we know these towers by their illumination in colour. These yellow, red, green, blue and white towers tell us the sector we are entering, and along the approach, light is used to see by and to give us direction.'

Expressways are like **RIVERS**

These **RIVERS** *frame the area to be served*

RIVERS *have* **HARBORS**

HARBORS *are the municipal parking towers*

from the **HARBORS** *branch a system of* **CANALS** *that serve the interior*

the **CANALS** *are the go streets*

from the **CANALS** *branch cul-de-sac* **DOCKS**

the **DOCKS** *serve as entrance halls to the buildings*

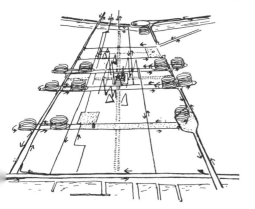

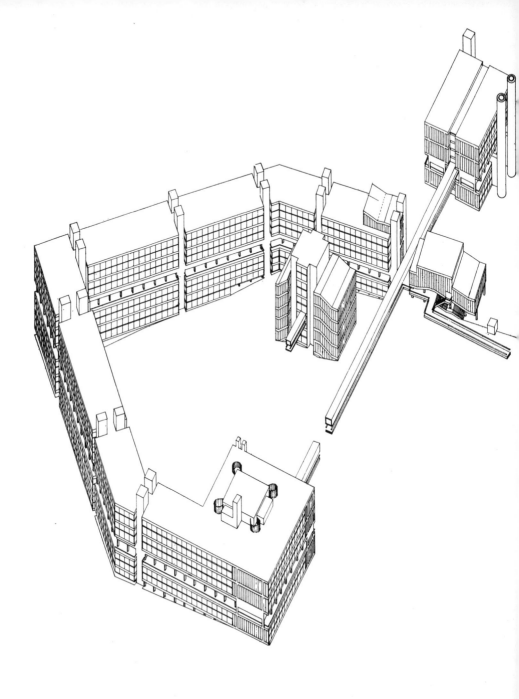

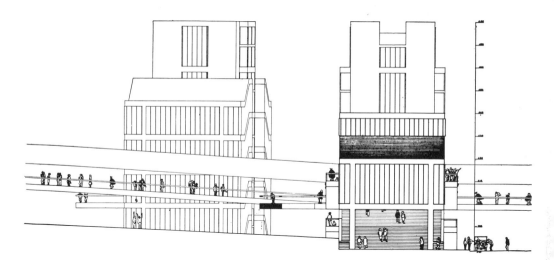

Sheffield University project: patterns of pedestrian movement are the key to the architectural organisation of the buildings

At a small urban scale, freedom to walk may be all that the situation demands or that can, in the economic balance, be provided and maintained.

This last problem—maintenance and the cleanliness of public circulation places once we have them—demands much forethought, for no one will want to pick up cigarette packets endlessly after a bunch of students.

In return for human protecting systems and spaces in a city will have to come a corresponding sense of responsibility for how they are used and kept looking inviting.

MOBILITY:
A DEMONSTRATION IN
UNIVERSITY OF SHEFFIELD
Extract from competition report, 1953

The key to any solution to the University of Sheffield lies in th
provision of a way across Western Bank. Without this link bein
forged, any development of university as a whole would be im
possible. The life of the university would be crippled by the segregatio
of the communal from the particular student activities.

A tunnel or bridge would not sufficiently stress the inter-dependenc
of the two sites and the two aspects of university life, for the lin
must be both a symbol and the generator of the whole complex.

For this reason we propose a new dominant—a high-level north
south link which will pass through the whole complex at the level c
the existing main entrance, linking the sites south of Western Ban
to those north of Western Bank, welding old and new buildings int
a unity.

And this north/south link is only part of a continuous high-lev
concourse from which all parts of the university can be reachec
Above this concourse is a complete service floor where all servic
runs and mechanical devices are located and maintained.

It is thus possible to keep the whole of the limited ground are
available free of circulation, and the park flows into the enclose
areas of the old and new buildings.

This method of high-level circulation can be likened to a ring-mai
whereby all students can equally readily and speedily gain full benef
from the closely-knit character of the university without congestin
the surrounding streets and dislocating that part of city life.

The new entrances to the university 'charge' this ring-main. The mai
north/south link will perform the function of an aqueduct carryin
both students and services to draw-off points.

The conception of high-level circulation and service in a continuou
building complex made it possible to satisfy the university's desi
to extend horizontally rather than vertically, in spite of the hug
volume of building to be put onto such a restricted site: for it wa
found that a traditionally planned Medical School dominated ar
destroyed whichever site it was placed upon, and that to build up
meaningful complex of separate buildings (one for each departmen
was impossible. Furthermore, the technological intention of muc
of the university seemed to point to buildings of the maximu
flexibility—so that today's laboratory can become tomorrow
testing room or studies. This flexibility is most easily achieved in
simple, repetitive, continuous structure.

On this particular site as the ground falls away to the east, the co
course level remaining constant, those departments with big spac
requirements (Chemistry and Medical School) have been located
the eastern part of the continuum, and those with relatively sma
space requirements (Arts, Administration and Physics) are in th

western part of the continuum. All these departments are accomodated in 'blockspace' for general purposes—offices, laboratories, workshops, etc., those things for which no high degree of identity is desirable. This 'block-space' is flexible both horizontally and vertically.

The Medical School has been deliberately chosen to form the anonymous enclosure of the greensward core of the university. Medical students, so long at the university compared with the majority of students, are also deliberately placed farthest from the Union and Refectory which they can most be relied upon to support; thronging the concourse level to and from the Library and Union they will keep the ring-main fully charged.

Those parts of the University with highly specialized functions have been given highly identified forms which punctuate and give point to the main continuum—the Arts Lecture Theatres and the Library Stacks on the north side, and communal activities of the south side.

The complex on the north site can best be described as a large snake curled round the site, whose head is the raised Arts Lecture Theatres which form the portico to the main entrance; the body, curving round the site is swollen by the bulk of the Medical School, and finally wraps its tail round the Library book-stack in a diminishing spiral. The north/south link lies like a stick behind its head and across its tail, pinning it to the ground.

MOBILITY:
A DEMONSTRATION IN
HAUPTSTADT BERLIN

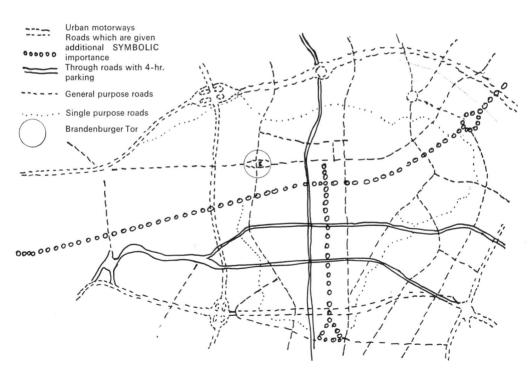

Urban motorways
Roads which are given additional SYMBOLIC importance
Through roads with 4-hr. parking
General purpose roads
Single purpose roads
Brandenburger Tor

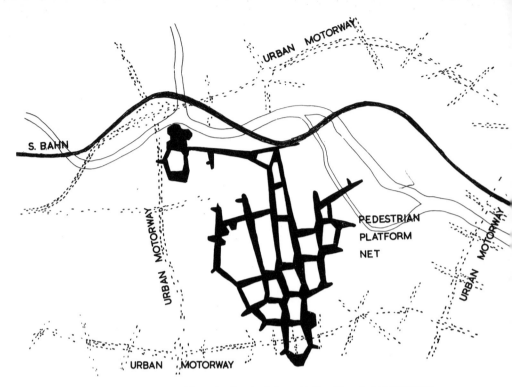

The pedestrian circulation net in its setting of urban motorways

Mobility has become the characteristic of our period. Social and physical mobility, the feeling of a certain sort of freedom, is one of the things that keeps our society together, and the symbol of this freedom is the individually owned motor car. Mobility is the key both socially and organizationally to town planning, for mobility is not only concerned with roads, but with the whole concept of a mobile fragmented, community. The roads (together with the main power lines and drains) form the essential physical infra-structure of the community. The most important thing about roads is that they are big, and have the same power as any big topographical feature, such as a hill or a river; to create geographical, and in consequence social, divisions. To lay down a road therefore, especially through built-up area, is a very serious matter for one is fundamentally changing the structure of the community.

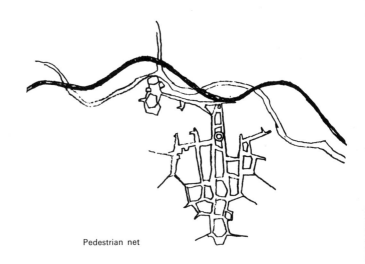

Pedestrian net

Traditionally some unchanging large-scale thing—the Acropolis, the River, the Canal, or some unique configuration of the ground—was the thing that made the whole community structure comprehensible and assured the identity of the parts within the whole.

Today our most obvious failure is the lack of comprehensibility and identity in big cities, and the answer is surely in a clear, large-scale, road system—*the 'URBAN MOTORWAY' lifted from an ameliorative function to a unifying function.* In order to perform this unifying function all roads must be integrated into a system, but the backbone of this system must be the motorways in the built-up areas themselves, where their very size in relationship to other development makes them capable of doing the visual and symbolic unifying job at the same time as they actually make the whole thing work.

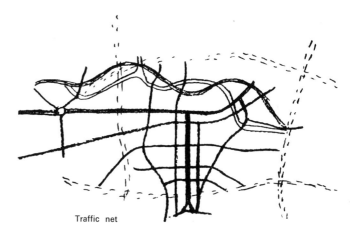

Traffic net

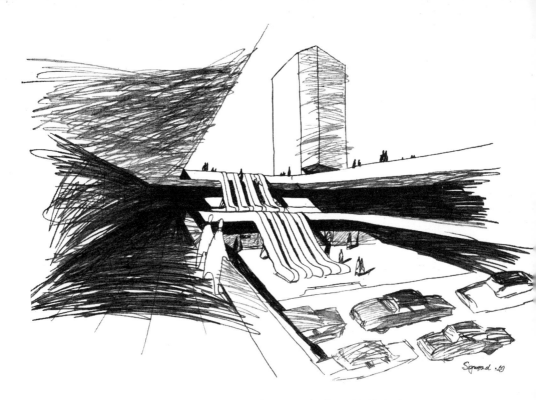

Interchange between pedestrian and traffic levels

To be physically positive the roads must run in a neutralized zone of
green planting or constructed landscape (whichever does the job
best).
The plan for the centre of Berlin is based on patterns of movement.
Much of the traffic load through the central area has been removed
by the tangential urban motorways and the proposed road system is
conceived in terms of leisurely driving and convenient parking. The
road net is right-angular (often following existing streets) with stop
lights at intersections and controlled crossings. It is accepted that
pedestrians and cars use the same level. But there is also a separate
system for pedestrians (and service trolleys) at a high level, running
on top of the low-spread buildings on the ground—the cinemas,
trade centres, markets, and so on. This high level pedestrian net
serves particularly the purely pleasure functions—shops, special

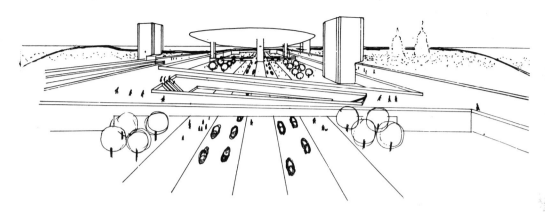

Friedrichstrasse, looking towards the Museum of Technology

lity markets, roof gardens, restaurants—but the main buildings on the ground—can also be reached from it.

The two systems are connected at points mid-way between each road intersection by continuously running escalators. These escalators make it easy to go from one level to the other and encourage the use of the platform level which bridges the road at the escalator points.

The geometry of the pedestrian platform is irregular (but not unsystematic), and emphasizes the much freer system of routes that is possible for a pedestrian than for vehicles. The rectangular road net, and the angular pedestrian platform, together form a pattern of spaces within which variations can be made, or buildings added, without destroying the basic concept.

Integrated with this system of low platforms are some high buildings

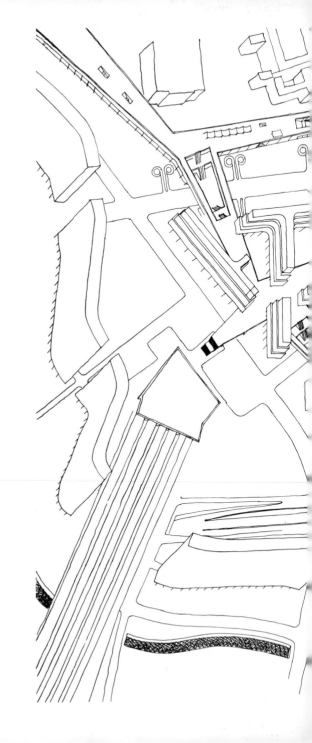

Southern portion Hauptstadt Berlin.
Drawing by Peter Sigmund.

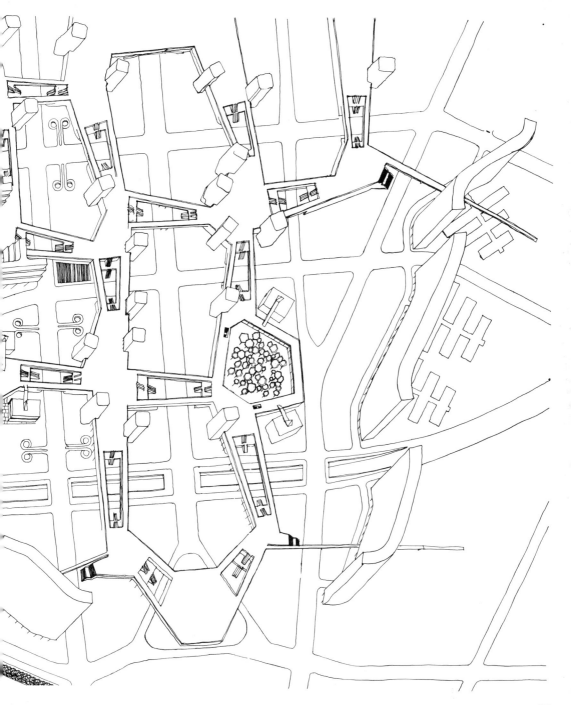

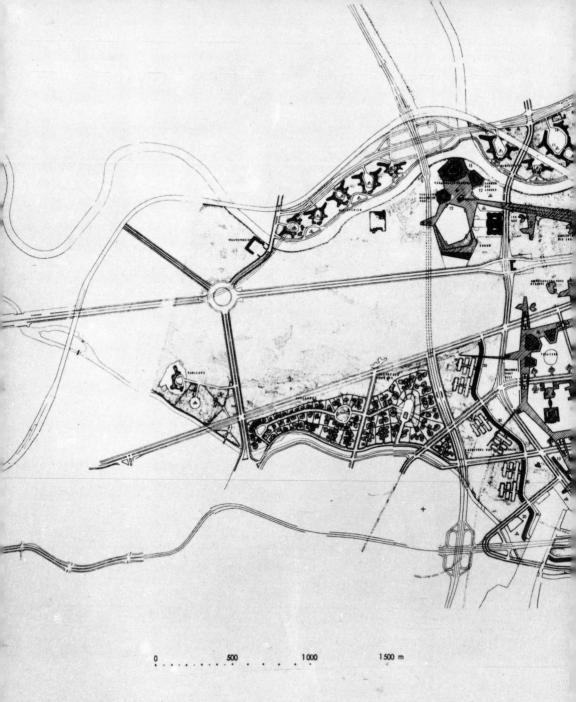

0   500   1000   1500 m

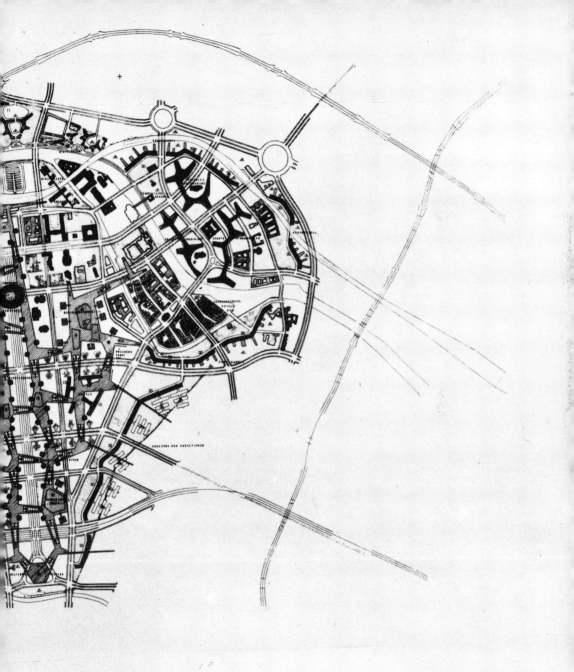

competition drawing Hauptstadt
Berlin A. P. Smithson and P.
Sigmonde.

Hauptstadt Berlin: central commercial centre in which a
separate pedestrian level is provided above the shops. This
pedestrian level reaches out into other sections of the city-
centre, for example, to the government area (top left). Drawing by Peter Sigmonde

—the administration of big shops, hotels, and so on—but most of the really big-volume buildings are on the periphery.

High buildings for business administration ring the pleasure city, with the government and local administration forming the boundaries to the north.

For each of these building types a general organizational principle has been evolved. Those buildings which are attached to the pedestrian level platform continue the theme of the platforms at various levels.

'This is a city in which every function has its own formal equivalent which is at once recognizable for what it is. Its organization is not rigid. The attempt has been made to create an open aesthetic, capable of variation and of growth, in which change cf social objectives can find an outlet.'

SUMMARY OF INTENTIONS OF LONDON ROADS

Firstly, PATTERNS OF MOVEMENT.
Although the roads system can be thought of *a priori* as a triangulated net of varying density (no hierarchy of routes, equal distribution cf traffic load over the whole net, equal accessibility to all parts, only one decision at each intersection, etc., etc.) the realities of the route finding and respect for (and wish to revalidate) the existing structure, as well as the desire to modify the town pattern generally, distort the net to a shape quite unlike any possible pre-conceptions. The resulting road net is not a pattern in the conventional formal sense, but is nevertheless a very real system to which the architecture must respond.

Secondly, ASSOCIATION.
Urban motorways can be so designed that they form the structure of the community. In order to work they must be based on equal distribution of traffic loads over a comprehensive net, and this system is by its nature apparent all over the community, giving a sense of connectedness and potential release. Furthermore, roads are the one big urban reorganization job which for practical and economic reasons must be carried out, and therefore money will be made available.

Thirdly, CLUSTER.

By increasing or decreasing the possibilities of communication the potential intensity of use can be manipulated. The increase of density of the traffic net in a given area will induce an increase in the use intensity in that area. The road net is therefore a tool to produce a change in the pattern—to break down the 'density pyramid' into a looser cluster of 'density points' (points of maximum intensity of use) with areas of lower residential density between; each area being more specific to its use than those allowed by present density blankets.

Fourthly, IDENTITY.

The roads can be deliberately routed, and the land beside them neutralized, so that they become obviously fixed things (that is, changing on a long cycle). The routing of individual sections over rivers, through parks, or in relation to historic buildings or zones, provides a series of 'fixes' or local identity points; the road net itself defining the zones identified by these 'fixes'.

Fifthly, PATTERNS OF GROWTH.

It is intended that the road structure should be more or less inviolable and protected by legislation as a 'fix'. New development would be conceived in terms of 'permanence' or 'transience', developing the theme of related cycles of change as the discipline of the architecture and town building.

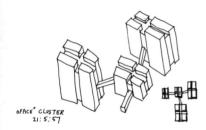

OFFICE CLUSTER
21: 5: 57

London Roads Study Team:
C. Dean, A. Eardley, R. Ballard, F. Baden-Powell, I. Fraser, J. Hunter

Opposite
Detail of centre of London Roads Study covering Bloomsbury/City

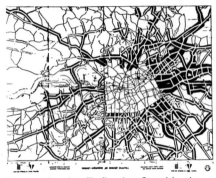

Diagram of peak traffic flow into Central London

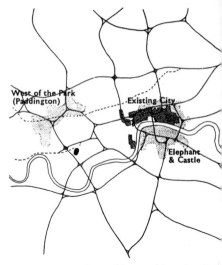

West of the Park (Paddington)

Existing City

Elephant & Castle

Areas of increased intensity of use

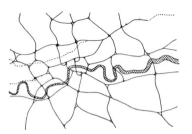

New network

LONDON ROADS STUDY

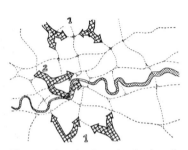

Diagrams of road pattern showing how the system distributes traffic

This study forms a practical exemplar of the interlocking town structure/architectural-form theories which we have gradually evolved during the past ten years.

It is founded on two basic tenets. The first (from Hounsfield) is that 'flow from every point to every other point . . . (is) best served by a net.'

The second is 'that a comprehensive system of urban motorways is the only thing capable of providing the structure for a scattered city.'

The disadvantages of a Hounsfield-type solution of a rectangular net are that all the junctions are four-way (too many decisions to be taken at a single point), and that in the central area, where the net has to be close, it is particularly destructive of the existing pattern of the city.

It is to overcome these disadvantages that in the London Roads Study the roads as they enter the built-up area, divide 'tangentially' into two. All the tangents from the various incoming roads ultimately interlock and become a net covering the whole built-up area. The pattern of the net is adjusted to respond to the existing structure of the city and is extended south and west to create new areas of intense use by providing communications where none now exist. The tangents from the incoming roads usually allow a decision to go to the centre or to go around it; but both roads are 'net roads': there is no question of 'through routes'.

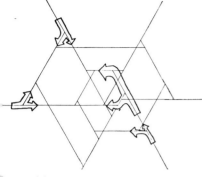

diagram of the system on which the road junctions are organized

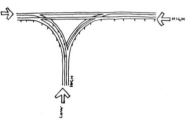

y road junction: only two choices, therefore no sitations

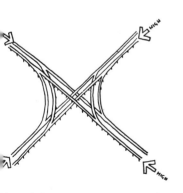

ht-angled motorway crossover on the same tem

Pages 64 and 65

London Roads Study: the new road network. The white line indicates where the existing radial system changes to a distributive network.

It is intended that the density and flow of the traffic should be the same all over the net. There is no hierarchy of importance, only a hierarchy of density. That is, where the use is greatest the road net is most dense. Were the road map lifted out of its context it should be possible to tell the areas of the most intense use from this alone.

The 'ideal' pattern of the new motorways (a triangulated net) has been modified by route-availability. Motorways follow cheap land adjacent to railways or, if necessary, are built over railways, previously unusable land such as marshes, or 'back land' routes. Junctions are sited on or over railway sidings or cheap property. Where junction space is not available the main routes just cross one another without interconnection and the junction is made elsewhere where space is available. The turn-off is achieved by doubling back, creating the characteristic 'dog ears' in the system around the old central area and the Elephant and Castle.

In general the new motorways are routed to avoid present areas of congestion, thus attracting traffic away from these points. (LCC* road improvements are integrated into the system, and are allowed for in the calculation of the total traffic capacity of the system.)

Architecturally the roads are intended to present a clear pattern in themselves and, as the same principles apply in different locations, it is hoped that in use the pattern will be apparent in spite of the many versions of junctions, take-offs, etc., that are necessary to meet the complex conditions of an existing city.

The motorways are routed to provide a series of 'identifying fixes' (places where a relationship to the city structure can be observed); for example, the route along the South Bank provides fixes on West-minster and the City, and the route across Hyde Park does the same in the central area.

Routing through the 'back-lands' is intended to help regenerate old areas by increasing land values This will happen especially around take-offs, where increased accessibility, garaging, pull-ins, hotels, service stations, etc., will provide new incentive to redevelopment. This is particularly so on the South Bank, which has never fully realized its potential because of bad communications. The deliberate re-routing of much of the traffic to and from the City from the west through the South Bank area creates a new zone of shopping, restaurants, entertainments, etc., for those people in transit as well as for the new resident office population.

* GLC since April 1965

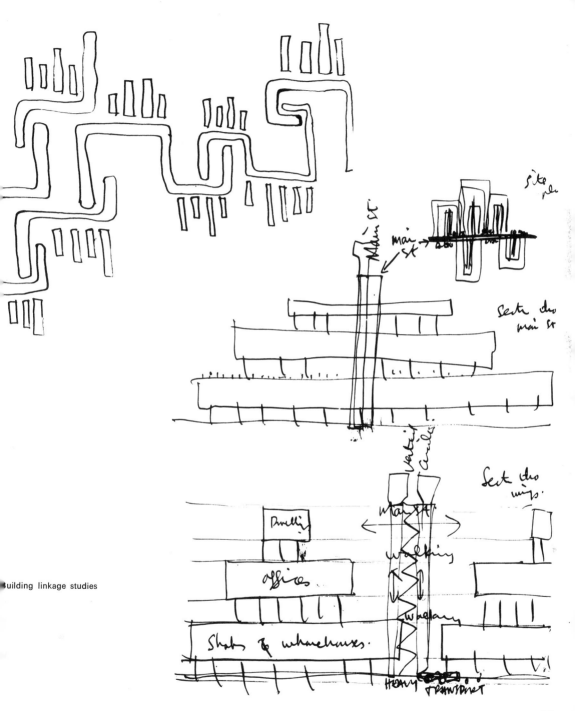

building linkage studies

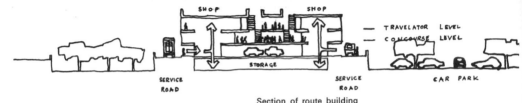

SHOP SHOP

━━━ TRAVELATOR LEVEL
─── CONCOURSE LEVEL

STORAGE

SERVICE
ROAD

SERVICE
ROAD

CAR PARK

Section of route building

NEW WAYS FOR LONDON

Soho Study:
C. Dean and B. Richards

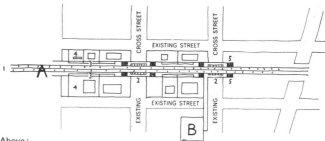

Above:

Plan of the route building. **A** *travelator* **B** *office tower*

Below:

Soho Study: the new motorway imposed upon the existing street pattern demands a change of scale in the redevelopment which must follow it. Motorway sections are linked by route buildings

SOHO STUDY

Any system of urban motorways introduces into the city a man-made element of an entirely new scale; the scale of geography. This scale seems to make the old sort of building totally inappropriate.

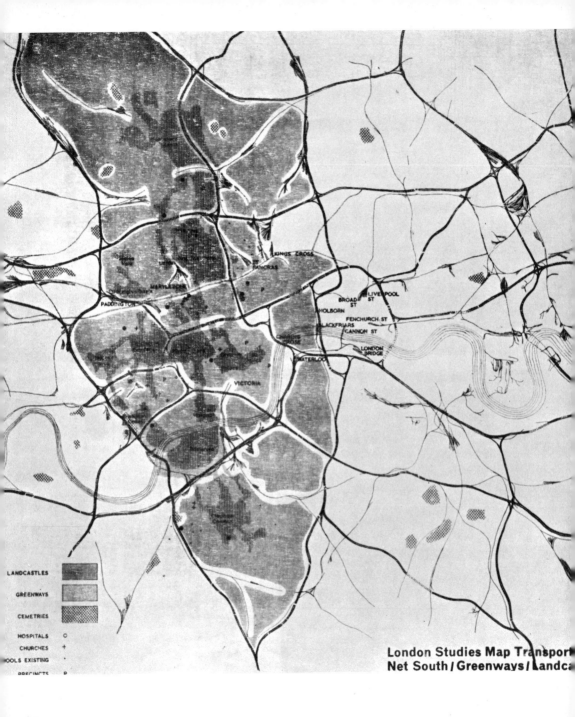

London Studies Map Transport
Net South / Greenways / Landca

LONDON STUDY:

GREENWAYS AND LANDCASTLES

In the diagram, the urban motorways of our London Roads Study 1959 are shown as if they existed. Out of this overlay of urban motorway net on the existing pattern of London, contrapuntal structuring systems have been extracted: derelict areas requiring ultimate total rebuilding related to big green landmarks (Landcastles), an open space linkage system to break the old pattern of traffic-bounded open spaces (Greenways). (A north-south Greenways structuring becomes apparent—interestingly similar to the north-south pattern of the Mars Group Plan for London.)

Greenways are needed to get about, in quiet, on foot, or on cycle. The diagram is made up of those routes that exist plus linkage through green squares and mews to new green strips plotted on marginal territory between industry and residential: to play a dual role of access greenway and buffer strip.

Schools and hospitals (which should both have more breathing space) are linked to it, and all housing has access to some part of the system.

Landcastles would have a new physical identity, taking over from the historical districts-in-name-only.

LONDON STUDY:

TRANSPORTATION NET SOUTH

South London is still much as it was built, and large areas of it require to be renewed or revalidated. This would be the time to take urban motorways through, creating new served and servant areas, before the spotting of new development compromises the situation.

The other obvious area open to re-structuring is in the arc from World's End round the north of the main line stations, to the river again east of Tower Bridge.

Were South and North London declared special re-structuring areas, the relief that an urban motorway net with its attendant servicing facilities would give to West End and City areas would enable, say in thirty years, the motorway net to be linked across them.

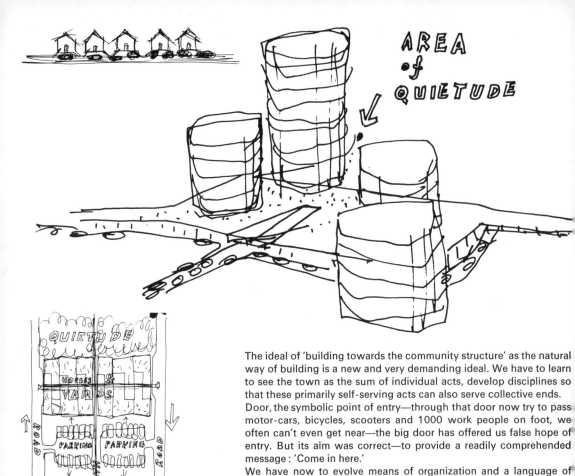

AREA
of
QUIETUDE

The ideal of 'building towards the community structure' as the natural way of building is a new and very demanding ideal. We have to learn to see the town as the sum of individual acts, develop disciplines so that these primarily self-serving acts can also serve collective ends.

Door, the symbolic point of entry—through that door now try to pass motor-cars, bicycles, scooters and 1000 work people on foot, we often can't even get near—the big door has offered us false hope of entry. But its aim was correct—to provide a readily comprehended message : 'Come in here.'

We have now to evolve means of organization and a language of equal obviousness for the new situations : 'Here I must walk in,' 'Here leave my car,' 'This way deliver the new machines.'

ON BUILDING TOWARDS

THE COMMUNITY STRUCTURE

Buildings should be thought of from the beginning as fragments; containing within themselves a capacity to act with other buildings; be themselves links in systems of access and servicing. This is the only viable mode of city-structuring : for all to develop a sense of structure.

For when a feeling of responsibility for the emergence of a structure is not there, an imposed structure cannot help.

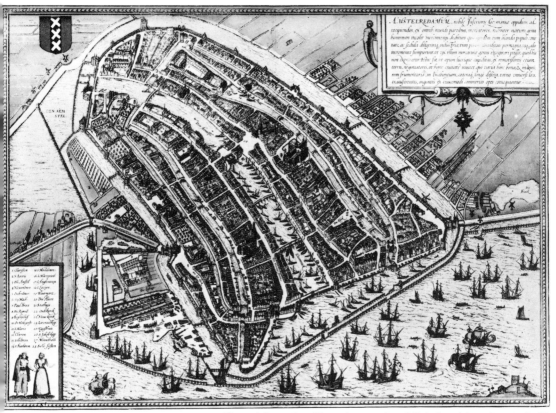

Plans of Amsterdam (sixteenth century) and Turin (late eighteenth century). 76

Our concern is for the poetry of movement, the sense of quietude, for the workplace to feel like a workplace, for the city of the machine to be able to be enjoyed with the same directness and deeply felt contentment we can still feel in the fishing harbour, the market place, the quayside, where older technologies and ways of doing things still hold.

To get a grip on the newer technologies in this sense is going to be a long process. But technological change is in fact relatively slow.

Los Angeles has been accepting the consequences of the car since the 1930's.

The Boeing 707 has been with us in embryo since the Superfortress, and looks like going on and on like the DC3 (which is [just] still with us).*

So it is no good saying that the speed of change makes it impossible for us to understand techniques in our bones in the old way, and to produce works of art.

The first DC3 flew on 22 Dec. 1935 over thirty years ago.

In Amsterdam the waterways are about 40 per cent of the built-up area, in Turin the fortifications with its 'cordon sanitaire' occupy more space than the built-up area.
The urban motorway net of a scattered city with its 'cordon sanitaire' and connections is likely to occupy about the same proportion of the total area as these.

This is the only thing that gives change meaning.
Cities are already too knitted-up and too dense; what they need to be loosened up, and the points of intensity of use spread about more, so that things can become themselves without so much artifice and struggle.
Compare the original openness and well-organization of Amsterdam or the old waterways of England with the clumsy system for the servicing of building today—with lorries backing and manoeuvring in inadequate spaces, with inadequate turning circles, often in dark and ill-ventilated basements. What pleasure can this give to the people who work there? It is asking men to work with poor tools. If 'systems of access' are to work sweetly 'to become themselves', develop their own disciplines, their own elegance, space is needed. For the scale of the motorized city is the scale of a city of great waterways, docks and harbours—an analogy made by Louis Kahn as part of his struggle to find an 'order of movement' for Philadelphia.

76

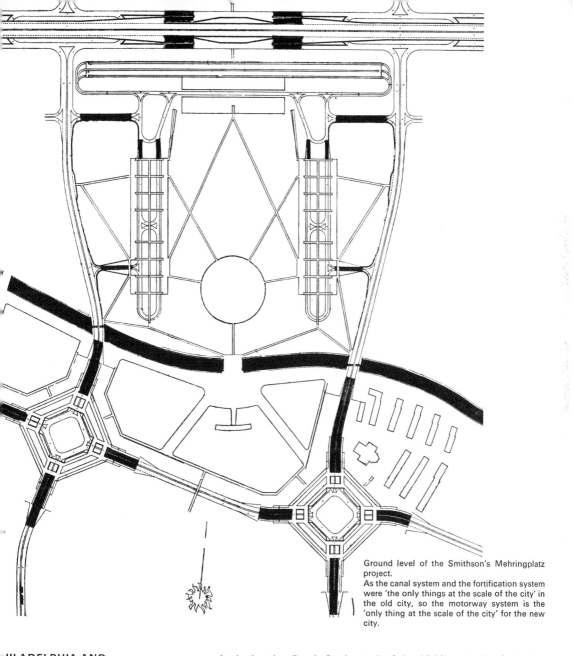

Ground level of the Smithson's Mehringplatz project.
As the canal system and the fortification system were 'the only things at the scale of the city' in the old city, so the motorway system is the 'only thing at the scale of the city' for the new city.

HILADELPHIA AND

HE LONDON ROADS

In the London Roads Study much of the thinking was dominated by Louis Kahn's Philadelphia Plan, the most important single contribution to changing our idea of the nature of the relationship between architect and urban planning that has yet been made.

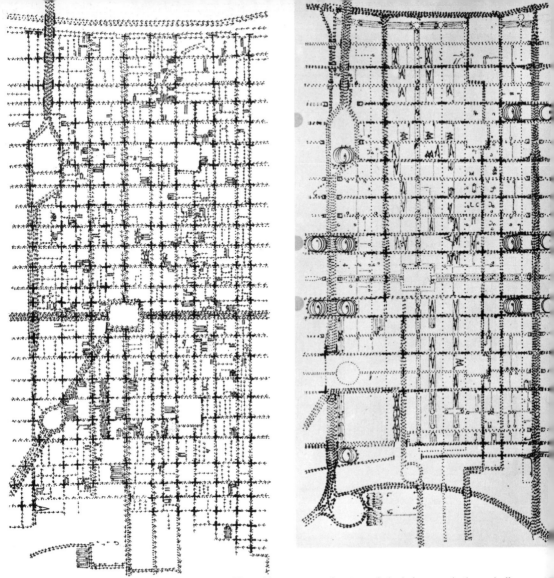

'The architect can control systems of physical communication and offer new co[n]cepts.'

This type of drawing made fifty years ago would show dots in all the streets— arrow, no crosses. The symbol of staccato movement would well have applied to [the] delivery wagon, carriage and horsedrawn trolley. Now on the same streets trolle[ys,] buses, trucks and cars with varying speeds, purposes and destinations travel togeth[er.] Uninterested traffic destined to places outside the centre may choose streets at w[ill.] Motion is further restrained by loading, deliveries and parking. Frequent intersecti[ons] frustrate movement.

Vine Street, widened to expressway dimensions, has the same number of intersecti[ons] as before. The original plans for the expressway which were not realized by [the] Philadelphia City Planning Commission called for a depressed cartway with entran[ce] by ramp to cross streets.

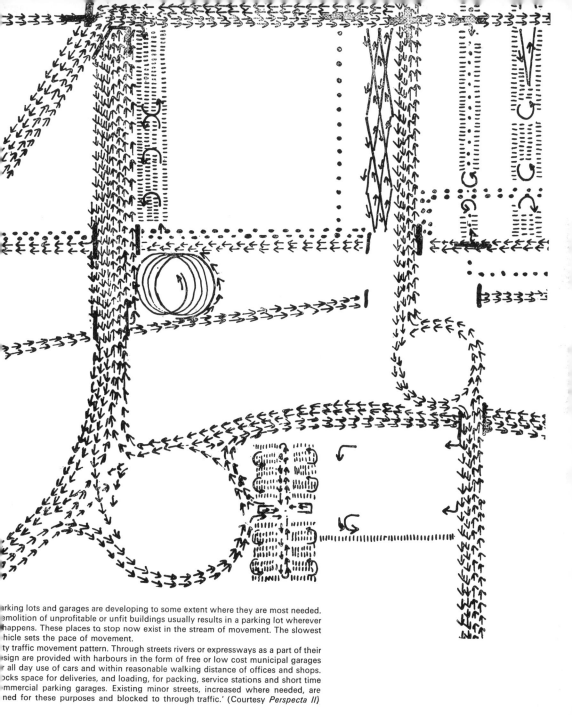

rking lots and garages are developing to some extent where they are most needed. emolition of unprofitable or unfit buildings usually results in a parking lot wherever happens. These places to stop now exist in the stream of movement. The slowest hicle sets the pace of movement.

ty traffic movement pattern. Through streets rivers or expressways as a part of their sign are provided with harbours in the form of free or low cost municipal garages all day use of cars and within reasonable walking distance of offices and shops. ocks space for deliveries, and loading, for packing, service stations and short time mmercial parking garages. Existing minor streets, increased where needed, are ned for these purposes and blocked to through traffic.' (Courtesy *Perspecta II*)

BERLIN: THE OPEN CITY

Berlin has what every other city in the world is beginning to wish it had—an open centre. In all the other metropolitan cities—with the exception of Los Angeles—development pressure has slowly brought about a condition of overbuilding. They are all cities kept in action by a vast deployment of mechanical devices . . . underground railway . . . lifts . . . escalators . . . travelators and so on, and by a layering of activities one above another . . ..

> apartments
> shops
> servicing
> parking
> etc.
> etc.

sustained by an equally vast deployment of air-conditioning and ventilating equipment and pipework generally.

For the ordinary user, enjoyment of the city tends to get squeezed out. The metropolitan cities have lost that sense of structure and feeling for use which we associate with the ordinary villages and towns of the past. It is the demonstrative and communicative function of architecture to provide such structuring, and such guidance, that we can use our cities as naturally and as unthinkingly as we breathe.

To get immediately to cases, let us take the question of the 'interchange'. In Paris, in London and in New York, the old main-line stations are being re-developed by the addition of 'commercial development'—office buildings, shops and so on. Now, traditionally the station spoke clearly, gave adequate guidance as to its use as TERMINAL . . . big engine hall as at King's Cross in London, or big concourse as at Grand Central in New York . . . but they are no longer 'terminals', they are 'interchanges'; and what is the shape of INTERCHANGE?

An interchange is a nodal event relating major transportation systems one to another.

Certainly we know that the transportation needs of the next half century will need more space, not less, than in the last half-century. And we know that in some way the direct servant functions of 'Interchange' . . . restaurants . . . hotels . . . meeting-spaces . . . shops . . . etc., have to be woven-in with the car-parking, taxi-ranks bus-terminals and underground entrances in such a way as to make clear what is going on, *and that these too will need space to make themselves clear, to work sweetly and not be so tightly knitted-up to be incapable of change.*

We are so used to overcrowding, we even accept it when presented as an ideal—an ideal of a layered-up city with servicing facilities and

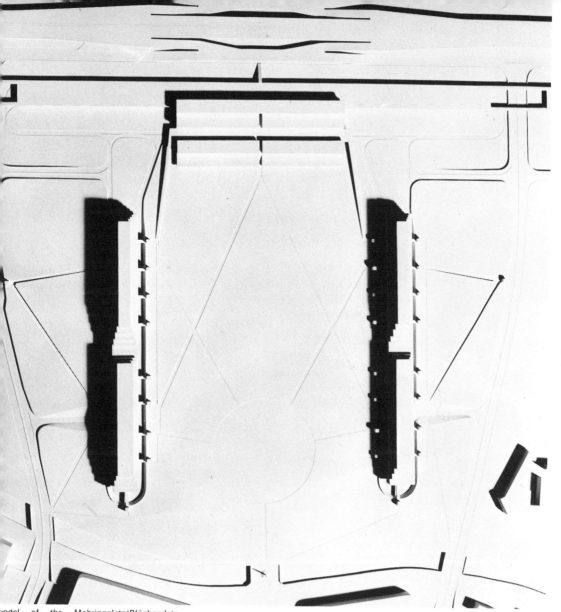

odel of the Mehringplatz/Blücherplatz
oject by Alison and Peter Smithson with
Nitschke.

circulation routes entirely below ground, permanently locked into the systems above. But few who have actually experienced life in the service area below State Street in Chicago, or in the parking shelters of Stockholm would voluntarily repeat the experience daily or opt to work there, as many people have to do to make them work.

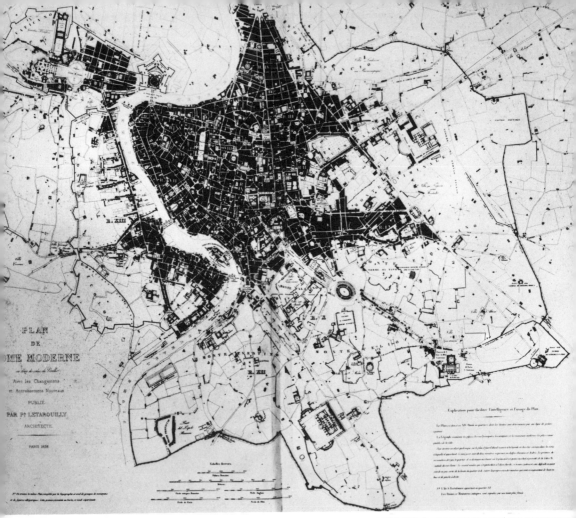

Plan of Rome in 1838 from L'Edifices de Rome Moderne. The plan reveals a gradual change in the structure after the final collapse of the Roman Empire. Renaissance princes built their large garden palaces and baroque public open spaces within the old walls, and thus restructured the old capital in a more open manner

Clear architectonic statement of the rights and pleasures of vehicular and pedestrian movement, and of quiet work place

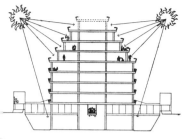

Section through 7-storey office building with roads
and servicing in moat below

Where now a minority are permanently below ground, soon we shall all live part of our lives in circulation sewers. And such systems of servicing and access, as systems, tend to be compromised geometrically and rendered inflexible by what goes on above—for example, by columns or bay sizes carrying down from above restricting turning circles, parking bay sizes, etc.

It is fundamental to system-building that sub-systems should be capable of change. In our discipline both the needs of human use and the needs of system growth demand space.

Berlin has space. She must use her present situation positively and build towards a new image of the metropolitan city.

An open city is nothing to be afraid of. Aristocratic cities in the past were like that—Jaipur or Karlsruhe for example, and so too was Rome

charoun's plan for Hauptstadt, Berlin. The Tier-
arten continues along the Unter-den-Linden and
ows around historical building groups at east end.
Hauptstadt Berlin – Karl Kramer 1960)

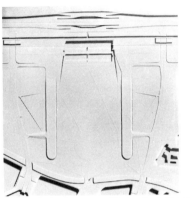

A relaxed, simple to use vehicular circulation system in free air, on and in the ground

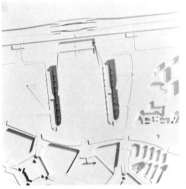

The simple buildings (83 see sectional Diagram)

right up to the end of the nineteenth century. When the Romans withdrew from England their towns were re-occupied in a new way with gardens and fields within the walls: and when Rome herself ceased to be the capital of the Empire, within her walls were built the villas and palaces of the Renaissance princes with their fabulous gardens, and the city was restructured in an entirely new and more open way. The availability of space was seized for a new sort of city.

What screams-out to be done in Berlin is to take similar advantage of the present situation. It is suggested :—

1. that the area adjacent to the Tiergarten and the area from the Mehringplatz up to the Wall, should be planted-up at once, as a simple grass and trees park, with certain of the roads closed to vehicular traffic.

2. that the idea of gradually getting back all the old street blocks by the spotting-down of single isolated buildings over the whole area should be abandoned, and a policy of grouping buildings into substantial clumps or 'landcastles' for the visual re-occupation of the centre be adopted.

3. that the new image of the central area would therefore be of park with big lumpish 'landcastles' around which servant activities would cluster.

4. that modern architecture of the 'Brazilia type, (such as at the Hansaviertel) would be unable to sustain such a concept, and that an architectural discipline more formally cohesive would need to grow with the general idea.

5. that, should the Anhalter-Bahnhof be re-developed, it would be an opportunity to create a real pioneer 'INTERCHANGE', related to the south-tangential road, to the U-bahn, to a general parking and service strategy such as was suggested in our Mehringplatz project.

6. finally, on the other side of the Wall, the areas alongside the Friedrichstrasse up to the Unter der Linden should be planted up as a park; the Tiergarten carrying straight on as in Scharoun's Hauptstadt plan with the historical buildings bedded into it. These buildings already have the sort of cohesive place-form we are searching for for the landcastles of new development and they would stand as a measure of our capacity to develop analogous new disciplines towards place-form.

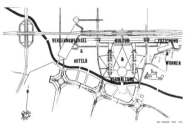

Events in the Mehringplatz area

Take off geometry at 650m intervals.

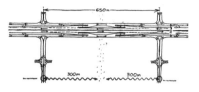

TOWN PLANNING ADVISORY
SCHEME AND REPORT FOR
MEHRING/BLÜCHERPLATZ,
BERLIN

General Principles

The problem of the Mehringplatz is how to be able to sense through the 'event' at this place the structuring of present-day Berlin, as one could sense through the old Belle Alliance Piazza the structure of Baroque Berlin. We propose the Mehringplatz area becomes an 'event' in a 'chain of events', following the line of the south tangential urban motorway.

Such a chain—a kind of linear centre—is a logical continuation of a natural tendency for the centre of Berlin to take an E-W linear form, (this tendency has been exaggerated by the division of the city into two zones).

The 'events' hung on to the south tangential urban motorway—are related to, and are symbols of, the zones through which the line of the motorway passes. For example:
related to the Anhalter Bahnhof, an 'interchange' with mass-transit facilities (bus, U-Bahn, car parking, hotels, etc.)
related to the 'Rund um die Kreuzkirche' housing there is a technical school complex.

We do not build-up these 'events' into a unified linear architectural 'composition': they are based on the same systems of connection and use-intensity zoning.

On both sides of the south tangential runs a continuous parking strip, varying in width and number of floors to suit need. At approximately 650m intervals are take-offs from which the 'events' and the areas they serve are reached. The basis of the 650m spacing is that:

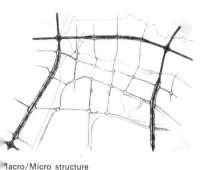

Macro/Micro structure

1. Three take-offs to the mile is standard American practice for down-town areas.
2. It is the minimum that the geometry of the take-off itself allows.
3. It produces a pattern giving a maximum walking distance of 300m.

The motorway grid forms the macro-structure, and the smaller grid of roads from the take-offs the micro-structure of each area.

The micro-structure roads follow in the main the old routes and serve the traffic needs within the super-blocks formed by the motorways. Where the micro-structure roads cross the motorways the take-offs are so designed as to invite the traffic onto the motorways for journeys longer than from one super-block to the next.

The road net is kept open, the maximum intensity of movement being along the motorway and at nodes where the car parks and service areas are located. The spacing of the micro-structure roads and nodes is based on a maximum walking distance of 300m. The centres of the blocks are kept free of vehicular movement.

Traffic movement pattern

Description of the arrangement within the Mehringplatz Aveu

North of the canal in the Mehringplatz area is located one of the 'events' which form the linear centre; south of the canal starts the normal micro-structure system with nodal car parks and servicing arrangements.

Along the south tangential runs the car park; onto this is hooked the 'facilities-building' (restaurant, shops, galleries, etc.); off the facilities building hang two banks of long, low administrative offices. Together, these enclose a green space (in a manner similar to the Louvre, and like the Louvre the whole would be realized serially), inside which there is no vehicular traffic. There is *NO* traffic at surface level anywhere within the block defined by the road net. The 'Victory monument is moved onto the Mehringbrücke to indicate that the bridge is no longer used for vehicular traffic. Along the motorway the linear garage forms a shield against traffic noise, and on the N-S roads the level of the ground is raised above road level for the same reason.

The rondel—a historical reminder of the Belle Alliance Rondel—is one of the points of origin of the footpath system: pedestrian traffic emanating from the Hallesches Tor U-Bahn station, the bus stops on the North-South roads, and the car parks.

The building is wide; on the office floors the central third is for computer, filing, conference rooms, etc., all that can function without natural light. This leaves the whole of the perimeter for normal offices.

The building stands on stilts in a waterless moat. Pedestrians reach the building across bridges, marked by interior neon-lit 'porticos'. The visitor would from here go to the vertical communication shaft behind each 'portico'. The main horizontal circulation would be along the 'gondola', suspended from the first floor over the void of the moat, with views out onto the central green space and down into the ever-changing activities of the moat service area—instead of along dreary between-office corridor of the normal administrative-type building.

Official cars would go straight to moat level, where there would be true 'port-cocheres' for VIP's, and lay-bys for official cars (on the inner side), as well as unloading bays for service vehicles (on the outer side). Private cars (except perhaps for cars of the disabled) would not be allowed into this area, but would be parked in the linear or nodal car parks, whichever is the nearest—never more than 300m from any entrance portico.

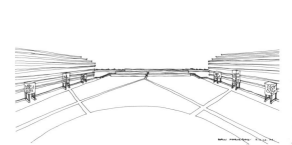

Mehringplatz, Berlin 1962

Elbow room

To keep the strict axial alignment of the Friedrichstrasse running through the Mehringplatz and across the Mehringbrücke we emphasise the symmetry of our building system around this original axis, letting the road system follow its own laws. In the central enclosed space, after the trees have grown up, it is intended that the presence of the buildings should hardly be felt at all. It is a deliberate strategy to leave space to give 'elbow room' for future change, and to give to vehicular movement the ease and elegance traditionally given, say, to movement between staircase and salon in a palace.

This feeling for increased 'elbow room'—for opening-up so that buildings, roads and services can each develop freely according to their own laws, and have the possibility of change without compromising the development as a whole, is central to our proposal. Our proposal is closer in spirit to Nancy (calm, urbane and even a little empty) than to most contemporary urban designs. The justification for such an 'aristocratic' use of space for such an ordinary problem is that if lack of crowding, calmness and quiet can be achieved, we have an obligation to use our increased productivity in this direction.

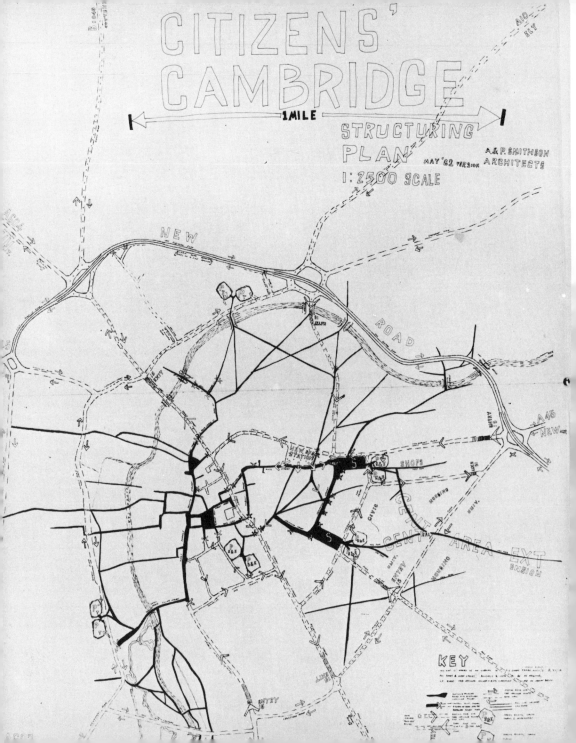

CITIZENS' CAMBRIDGE

1MILE

STRUCTURING
PLAN MAY '82 VERSION A.&P. SMITHSON ARCHITECTS

1:2500 SCALE

NEW

ROAD

KEY

CITIZENS' CAMBRIDGE :

A PLANNING STUDY

This is a study undertaken to try to discover a general 'structuring' strategy which would allow for the continuing existence of the historic centre and permit of its enjoyment (Cambridge is a 'world city' comparable with Kyoto or Amsterdam), at the same time as ensuring its continuing viability as a living University and regional town. The problem is primarily one of Preservation and the Removal of Pressure. The built-form of the historical centre of Cambridge is incapable of accepting new traffic routes, or large unit enterprises (with their necessarily enlarged scale of building and servicing and parking arrangements). The historic centre must, in fact, be regarded as one big building, and a preservationist attitude adopted towards it. To achieve this :—

(a) A central area extension must be created within walking distance of the old centre, which is capable of dealing with present-day regional scale shopping and parking needs. This extension would not be a pure 'shopping centre', but would continue the existing Cambridge central area mixture of alternating commercial, civic and university facilities, and housing. Existing housing groups being retained where these have qualities capable of sustaining themselves in a new context. How exactly this can be achieved—new big scale, new transportation, new noise, higher density of use : against old domestic scale and old privacy—remains the key problem, as yet untouched.

The creation of this new area would take the pressure off the old centre, enabling the low-rental traditional small shops to survive, and some houses now used as shops would be returned to domestic use.

(b) The existing extensive footpath systems would be extended by the closing off of certain streets to vehicular traffic during peak pedestrian and bicycle hours; these pedestrian routes to be served by buses from the suburbs (where similar footpath systems could be established) passing clockwise and anti-clockwise around the centre.

It has been recognized in Legislation only perhaps in France that groups of buildings which make a distinctive 'place' are as much worthwhile protecting intact as individual architectural features.

What constitutes a good environment, apart from 'the smell in the air'—a place that is good to live in?

Conservation could have a real freeing power in our cities. By conserving intact for periods of twenty or forty years such areas that still offer viable human environment, there could be established 'fixes' which would cut the field of action for creative planning down to manageable size. The conserved area-fixes would be continual reminders of the right scale of thinking, elucidating at all stages the elusiveness of 'good environment'. Area-fixes would tend to channel creative planning into areas whose environment has been totally invalidated.

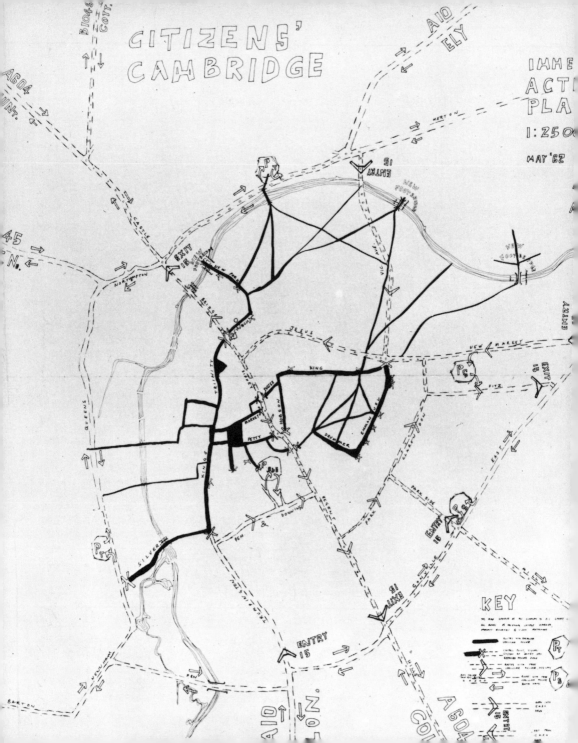

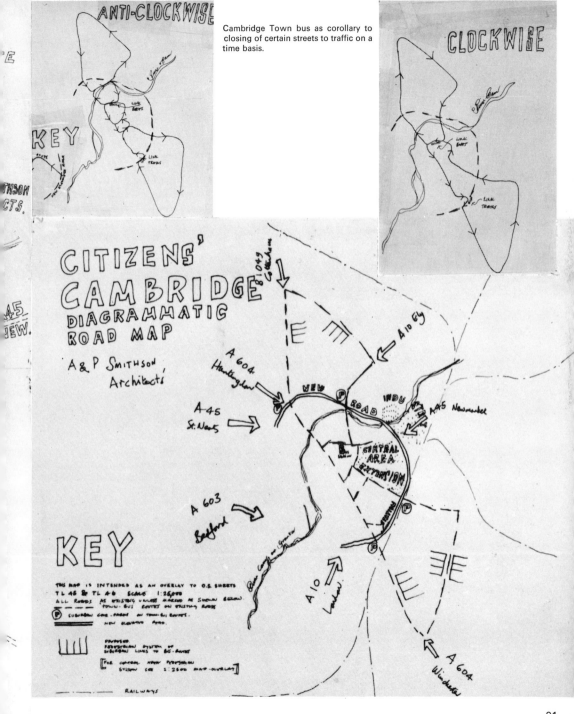

Cambridge Town bus as corollary to closing of certain streets to traffic on a time basis.

ANTI-CLOCKWISE

CLOCKWISE

CITIZENS' CAMBRIDGE DIAGRAMMATIC ROAD MAP

A & P Smithson, Architects'

KEY

(c) Cars would be free to use most of the existing street system, but would be discouraged by the no-through one-way routing and restricted parking. Cross town journeys would be made along a short urban motorway outside the historic centre. This motorway would serve direct into the car parks of the new central area extension. There would be one central area car park to serve the old town, and fringe car parks for tourists and all-day parkers. All these car parks would be linked directly into the footpath system.

STREET: SOMERSET, ENGLAND

In the summer of 1964 we were asked—to advise on the most appropriate new use for a site in the High Street now occupied by Crispin Hall—a community hall built in the nineteenth century, now falling into disuse. Looking into the problem it became obvious that in order to give an answer the general structure of Street would have to be examined. A town–structure study was made, and there emerged three obvious town needs:

1 for a town-service road which would allow the High Street to return to its original town distributor role,

2 for the development of the Crispin Hall site as part of the central 'social strip', linked to the new central car parks and to the existing, but now fragmented, footpath system.

3 for the prevention of any further housing growth on the existing pattern of estate roads one following the other, a process that is obliterating the alternating 'open space and then buildings' which with the separation of roads and footpaths, is the very pleasant 'as found' pattern of Street, and for the selection of new areas for housing development where the continuation of this 'as found' pattern would be possible.

Eastside of Crispin Hall looking from High Street corner.

Existing Crispin Hall and High Street

As architects we hope to control the design of the town-service road; build a re-orientating shopping and social needs complex on Crispin Hall site; and build a pilot-operation housing group in a new housing area. By touching Street at the three most useful points, we hope to raise, by example, the level of consideration for the continuation of Street as a place.

Our intention being to try to renew in Street that feeling of living in a small country town.

We have gradually come to the understanding that this feeling is largely generated by the presence of farming and other open land within the town which brought rural activitities into the town's life and gave it an open texture of alternating quiet and active areas.

The feeling is also due to the town's actual size—in a town very much bigger than Street the sense of country (smell, bird life, etc.) would sharply diminish (Present population, 7000).

All our proposals are therefore modest. They have an open texture with extensive use of footpath access, especially for children going to school and to local shops. Good fields are to be kept, new housing and planting to be in dullish areas which needed enlivening.

Rear street of Crispin site

Remains of footpath system at the side of Crispin site

Overleaf
Town map for Street with the feeling of penetration of countryside shown as arrows.

93

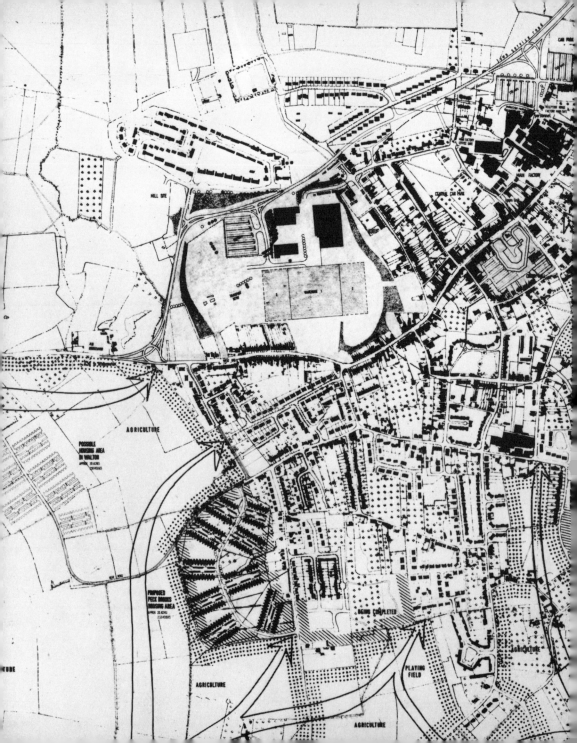

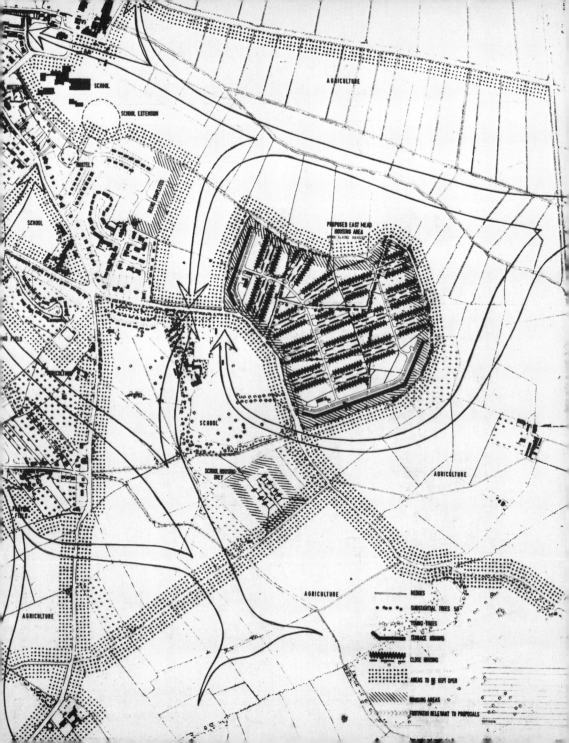

AGRICULTURE

SCHOOL

SCHOOL EXTENSION

HOSTEL

SCHOOL

PROPOSED EAST MEAD
HOUSING AREA

SCHOOL

SCHOOL HOUSING
ONLY

AGRICULTURE

PLAYING
FIELD

AGRICULTURE

AGRICULTURE

AGRICULTURE

HEDGES

SUBSTANTIAL TREES

YOUNG TREES

TERRACE HOUSING

CLOSE HOUSING

AREAS TO BE KEPT OPEN

HOUSING AREAS

FOOTPATHS RELEVANT TO PROPOSALS

The first aim was to offer a wide choice of home types. The homes for sale to car owning workers in a small town. The solution here is in growth groups, each like a flower.

The building rate is slow. Each part would be put up by a local builder as one operation. The pattern of the houses fitted to the contours, the view of the fields; leaving unharmed many big trees. This study is a composite print of two of the many made.

The principal new fact that emerged in subsequent discussion of the new housing area was that the proportion of middle class houses to ordinary houses was 1 : 135. The new housing area needs therefore to be predominantly of the £3000 to £4/5000 type of house. In the latest version (previous page).

The houses shown are a development of the 'Close Houses' idea, linked into a general loop road and footpath system.

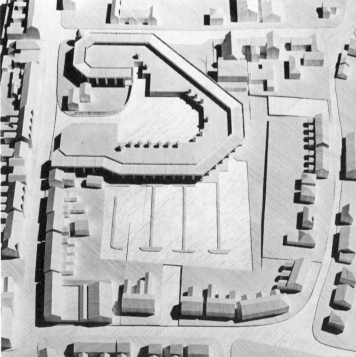

Crispin Hall, outward looking shopping groups. Safe finger access from car park and safe foot path from the housing areas adjacent. Service yard in the centre.